T0053085

THE
DOLLAR
BILL

in Translation
What It Really Means

Revised Edition

by Christopher Forest

CAPSTONE PRESS
a capstone imprint

Fact Finders is published by Capstone Press,
1710 Roe Crest Drive, North Mankato, Minnesota, 56003
www.mycapstone.com

Library of Congress Cataloging-in-Publication Data is available on the Library of Congress Website

    ISBN: 978-1-5157-6249-2 (revised paperback)
    ISBN: 978-1-5157-6233-1 (ebook pdf)

Editorial Credits
Megan Schoeneberger, editor; Gene Bentdahl, designer and illustrator; Wanda Winch, photo researcher

Photo Credits
AP Images: Hillery Smith Garrison, 24
Capstone Press: 21 (all); Capstone Studio: Karon Dubke, Cover Top, 4 Background, 5 Bottom, 6 (all), 8 (all), 10 (all), 12 (all),
13 (all), 14 Back, 14 Top Left, 14 Top Right, 16 (all), 18 Left, 18 Top, 18 Middle, 20 Background, 25
iStockphoto: Samuel Borges, Cover Bottom; Library of Congress: Prints & Photographs Division, 9 Bottom Left, 9 Bottom
Right
National Parks Service: Colonial National Historical Park, 20
North Wind Picture Archives: 14
Shutterstock: Bruce Stanfield, 18 Bottom, Donna Ellen Coleman, 15, michaeljung, 28, Orhan Cam, 5 Top, Shipfactory, 9 Top
The Currency House Inc: www.thecurrencyhouse.com, 22, 23 top, 23 Bottom

Design Elements: Capstone Studio: Karon Dubke

Essential content terms are defined at the bottom of the page where they first appear.

Table of Contents

CHAPTER 1

The Mysterious Dollar Bill

There's a mystery in your pocket. Or maybe it's in your wallet or hidden away in your sock drawer.

Need some clues? It's not a book, but it does tell a story. It's full of secret codes, puzzling pictures, and hidden meanings.

You may have one or two or hundreds of them. No matter how many you have, you probably want more. Yet most of the time you give it away almost as soon as you get it.

What is it?

BUREAU OF ENGRAVING AND PRINTING

The Bureau of Engraving and Printing prints dollar bills and other U.S. money.

front side of the U.S. dollar bill

back side of the U.S. dollar bill

It's a dollar bill. You know, that crumpled piece of paper you got for your allowance last week. Or did you spend it already?

The next time you have a dollar bill, don't just rush out and buy something. Hold on to it for a while. Look closely at your dollar. What do all those strange numbers mean? Since when do pyramids have eyes? What in the world does "Annuit Coeptis" mean? Is that even English?

See? It's way more than a dollar bill. It's a mystery.

Some parts of the dollar bill tell stories of America's history. Codes tell when and where the bill was printed. There's a lot of information printed on a simple dollar bill. But everything is there for a reason.

What do these words and symbols mean? Turn the page to take a closer look.

CHAPTER 2

The Dollar Bill Up Close

WASHINGTON

What?

A **picture** of **George Washington** is on the front of the dollar bill.

Washington's picture on the dollar is based on a famous 1796 portrait by Gilbert Stuart.

Washington's face isn't the only one to show up on the dollar bill. The first dollar bill showed a picture of Salmon P. Chase. He was the secretary of the treasury in 1862, when the first dollar was printed.

Federal Reserve Note

THIS NOTE IS LEGAL TENDER FOR ALL DEBTS, PUBLIC AND PRIVATE

Legal Tender

Seal of the Department of the Treasury

Who Signed My Dollar Bill?

If you look on either side of Washington, you will see signatures. The signature on the right belongs to the secretary of the treasury. This person is in charge of the Department of the Treasury. The signature on the left is the name of the treasurer of the United States. The treasurer oversees money manufacturing. Both signatures must appear on the bill to make it legal.

note — paper money, not coins

legal tender — money that the government issues for paying debts

10

Federal Reserve Note:

This paper money was issued by the U.S. government's central **bank**.

Legal Tender:

You can use this dollar bill to pay for something.

Seal of the Department of the Treasury:

The **seal** shows that the Department of the Treasury, founded in 1789, made this dollar bill. The Department of the Treasury is the agency responsible for printing money in the United States.

The Federal Reserve System oversees the U.S. banking system. The Bureau of Engraving and Printing prints all U.S. paper money for the Federal Reserve. Twelve Federal Reserve Banks and their branches distribute the money.

There are many symbols on the seal. The scale represents justice. The 13 stars stand for the original 13 colonies that made up the United States. People don't agree on what the key stands for. Some people say it stands for the key to open the Treasury. But the Department of the Treasury says it symbolizes the Treasury's power and authority.

Federal Reserve Seal

note position number

What?

Federal Reserve Seal:

This bill **was issued** by the Federal Reserve Bank in Minneapolis, Minnesota.

Note Position Number:

This code shows the position of the bill on the plate from which it was printed.

The letter on the seal tells you which of the 12 Federal Reserve Banks issued the bill.

A: Boston   E: Richmond   I: Minneapolis
B: New York   F: Atlanta   J: Kansas City
C: Philadelphia   G: Chicago   K: Dallas
D: Cleveland   H: St. Louis   L: San Francisco

I 60953601 A

serial number

FW A 5

note position letter and
plate serial number

SERIES
2006

series year

Serial Number:

The serial number tells which number the bill was on a production run. The first letter matches the Federal Reserve Seal. The last letter shows what groups of bills **this bill** was printed with.

Note Position Letter and Plate Serial Number:

This **code** shows which plate was used to print the dollar bill.

Series Year:

The **design** for this bill was first used in 2006.

There are between 7.5 billion and 9 billion $1 bills in circulation at one time.

The FW means the bill was printed in Fort Worth, Texas. If your dollar bill doesn't show FW, it was printed in Washington, D.C.

If there is a small change to the dollar's design, the series year is changed.

13

IN GOD WE TRUST

In God We Trust

8

plate serial number

The motto "In God We Trust" recognizes early American settlers' strong belief in God. This faith guided them in the creation a new government.

What?

In God We Trust:

"In God We Trust" is the official <u>motto</u> of America.

Plate Serial Number:

This number identifies which plate was used to print the back of this dollar bill.

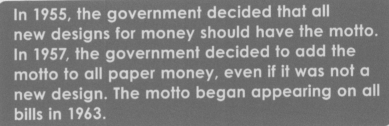

In 1955, the government decided that all new designs for money should have the motto. In 1957, the government decided to add the motto to all paper money, even if it was not a new design. The motto began appearing on all bills in 1963.

Seeing Green

The green ink on a dollar bill is no ordinary ink. The government keeps the ingredients in the ink top secret. That way, no one can make their own ink to print fake bills. But why green? No one really knows. Most likely, when money was first printed, green ink was probably easiest to find.

The Dollar Bill Continued

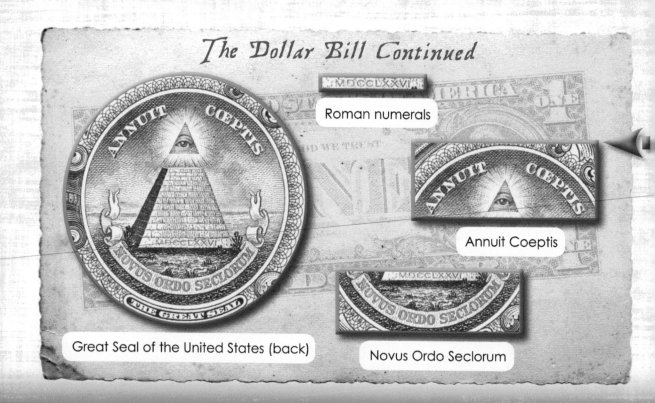

Roman numerals

Annuit Coeptis

Great Seal of the United States (back)

Novus Ordo Seclorum

The Mysterious Seal

The U.S. government hasn't explained why the pyramid on the Great Seal is unfinished. But some people think it represents the idea that America is always growing. The eye is called the "all-seeing eye." There are many legends about what it means. According to one legend, the eye looks left so that it is gazing to the west. This might symbolize how the country expanded west in order to grow. But the eye most likely stands for the powers that guided the United States when it was first becoming a country.

16

Great Seal of the United States (back):

This is the back side of the seal.

Roman Numerals:

These <u>Roman numerals</u> say <u>1776</u>.

Annuit Coeptis:

This Latin phrase means "He has favored our undertaking."

Novus Ordo Seclorum:

This is another Latin phrase. It means "a new order of the ages." It refers to the time that began after 1776, when America declared its independence.

These letters aren't some secret code. They are Roman numerals, which use letters to stand for numbers.

In 1776, leaders of the 13 Colonies signed the Declaration of Independence.

The Dollar Bill Continued

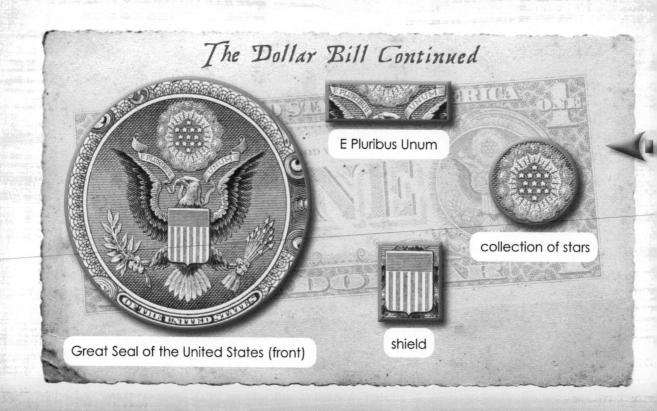

E Pluribus Unum

collection of stars

shield

Great Seal of the United States (front)

What's Up with 13?

You see the number 13 a lot on a dollar bill. There are 13 arrows, 13 leaves in the olive branch, 13 stars, and 13 stripes on the shield. You may think 13 is an unlucky number, but in this case, it isn't. The number stands for the original 13 colonies that formed the United States.

1776 colonial flag

Great Seal of the United States (front):

This is the front side of the Great Seal. The eagle is an official symbol of America. In its left talons, the eagle holds an <u>olive branch</u>. This is a symbol of peace. The arrows in the eagle's right talons stand for war.

E Pluribus Unum:

This Latin phrase means "one out of many." It refers to America, which is one country made of many states.

Collection of Stars:

The collection of stars illustrates the United States taking its place among other countries.

Shield:

The shield has nothing holding it up. This suggests that America can succeed by following its own beliefs.

On the Great Seal, the eagle faces the side with the olive branch. Many people say that having the eagle face the olive branch shows that America tries to stay peaceful.

CHAPTER 3

How the Dollar Bill Came to Be

Before America became a country, colonists did not have paper money. They used animal skins, farm products, and other goods to trade for what they needed. In 1652, the Massachusetts Bay Colony became the first colony to make coins. At that time, making coins was against British law. In 1690, Massachusetts also began making paper money called bills of credit.

Pennsylvania, 1773

Rhode Island, 1780

Continental currency, 1778

South Carolina, 1778

During the Revolutionary War (1775–1783), each state issued paper money. As the war got more expensive, states printed more money. Soon, so many notes were printed that they were almost worthless. States stopped issuing paper money for widespread use.

By the end of the war, the U.S. money system was a mess. Finally in 1789, Congress formed the Department of the Treasury to manage money in the United States. In 1792, Congress made the dollar the basic unit of U.S. money. It also set up a national mint in Philadelphia. The mint made $10 gold coins, silver dollars, and other coins.

mint — a place where coins are made

The dollar bill first appeared as a type of money in 1862. That year, America was fighting the Civil War (1861–1865). The government decided to print paper money called greenbacks or national currency. The greenbacks were rather large and not popular at first. But in time, Americans accepted the paper money.

Over the years, the design changed slightly. In 1929, the Department of the Treasury decided to make the bills smaller. The smaller size saved on printing costs. Today a dollar bill is 2.625 inches (6.6675 centimeters) from top to bottom. It measures 6.125 inches (15.5575 centimeters) from left to right.

front of greenback

back of greenback

More changes were to come. In 1935, both sides of the Great Seal of the United States were added to the back of the dollar bill. In 1963, the words "In God We Trust" were also added to the back side. The 1963 design has been used ever since.

1917 dollar bill

1923 dollar bill

Making Money

The Department of the Treasury designs and prints U.S. money. The department does this through the Bureau of Engraving and Printing. The Bureau of Engraving and Printing prints all American paper money.

Printing a dollar bill takes more than 65 steps from start to finish. Engravers start by cutting the bill's design into a steel plate. This plate is used to create a printing plate. Next the Bureau of Engraving and Printing sends large sheets of paper through a high-speed press.

The dollar bill, like all American paper money, is printed on large sheets of paper. The paper is a special blend of cotton, linen, and red and blue fibers. This blend makes the bills strong. The fibers also make it hard for anyone to copy the bills.

Each sheet of paper holds 32 bills. The sheets are then cut into individual bills. Then they are shipped to Reserve Banks, which distribute them to commercial banks. A typical one-dollar bill lasts anywhere between 18 and 21 months in circulation. Then it is removed from circulation, shredded, and recycled.

Money Matters

Dollar bills are the most common kind of notes in the United States. Almost half of all the bills the Bureau of Engraving and Printing prints are dollar bills. The dollar bill has changed in shape, size, and design. But it continues to be an important reminder of the history of America. And now that you know the history, you'll never look at money the same way again.

A taler, a type of silver coin, is first minted. This German word is the basis for the word dollar.

George Washington appears on the dollar note for the first time.

1518

1869

1862

1928

The U.S. government issues the first dollar note. It has a picture of then Secretary of the Treasury Salmon P. Chase.

The Department of the Treasury selects the portraits that should appear on paper currency. They begin appearing on bills the following year.

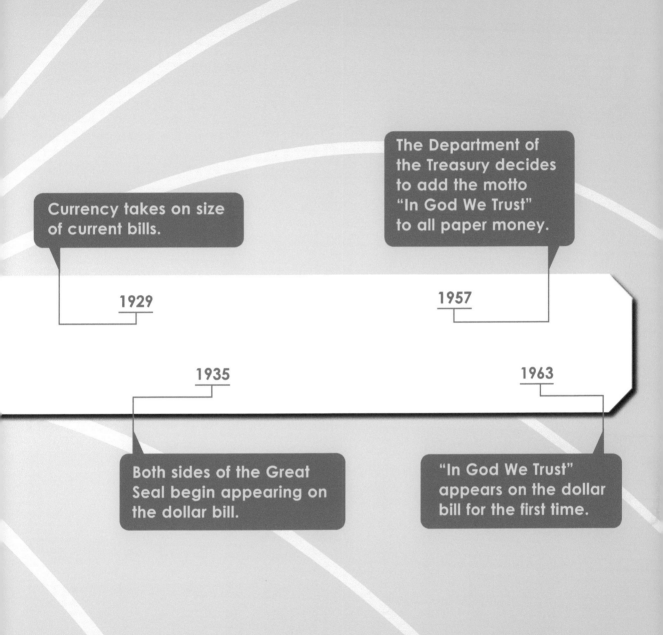

Currency takes on size of current bills.

The Department of the Treasury decides to add the motto "In God We Trust" to all paper money.

1929

1957

1935

1963

Both sides of the Great Seal begin appearing on the dollar bill.

"In God We Trust" appears on the dollar bill for the first time.

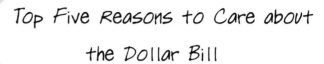

Top Five Reasons to Care about the Dollar Bill

5. The dollar bill is money. And, like all money, it is valuable.

4. The dollar bill is a collector's item. Many people collect coins and dollar bills. It is a fun way to learn about money and the stories it has to tell.

3. The dollar bill has stood the test of time. It has been a popular form of money for more than 145 years.

2. The dollar bill is a piece of history. It reminds people why America became a country. The symbols on the bill show the reasons why America wanted to be free.

1. The dollar bill is not just money. It is a symbol of America. The dollar itself reflects America's history. It has grown and changed along with America.

Translation Guide

<u>**Annuit Coeptis**</u> — Is this a hero in a science fiction movie? No, this 13-letter phrase is Latin for "He has favored our undertakings."

<u>**Department of the Treasury**</u> — This isn't where pirates hide treasure. It's the department of government that is responsible for printing currency or collecting taxes.

<u>**E Pluribus Unum**</u> — It sounds like some kind of public transportation. But this 13-letter motto means "Out of many, one" in Latin.

<u>**Great Seal**</u> — No, this isn't a zoo animal that performs really cool tricks. The Great Seal of the United States is a symbol used on important government documents.

<u>**Novus Ordo Seclorum**</u> — This isn't a magic spell. It is Latin for "new order of the ages."

Glossary

circulation (sur-kyuh-LAY-shuhn) — use or passage from person to person or place to place

Federal Reserve Note (FED-ur-uhl re-ZURV NOHT) — the only kind of paper money that is legal in the United States

legal tender (LEE-guhl TEN-dur) — money that the government issues for paying debts

mint (MINT) — a place where coins are made

note (NOHT) — a piece of paper money

portrait (POR-trit) — a picture of a person usually showing the face

production run (pruh-DUHK-shuhn RUHN) — bills printed at one time using a set of serial numbers

serial number (SIHR-ee-uhl NUHM-ber) — a number that identifies a bill

Internet Sites

FactHound offers a safe, fun way to find educator-approved Internet sites related to this book.

Here's what you do:

1. Visit *www.facthound.com*
2. Choose your grade level.
3. Begin your search.

This book's ID number is 9781429627948.

FactHound will fetch the best sites for you!

Read More

Adler, David A. *Money Madness.* New York: Holiday House, 2009.

Bailey, Gerry, and Felicia Law. *Cowries, Coins, Credit: The History of Money.* My Money. Minneapolis: Compass Point Books, 2006.

Clifford, Tim. *Around the World with Money.* The Study of Money. Vero Beach, Fla.: Rourke, 2009.

Hall, Margaret. *Money.* Earning, Saving, Spending. Chicago: Heinemann, 2008.

Index